Foraging for Wild Food in England
Spring Edition

OTHER BOOKS FROM GAVIN IRELAND AND FOUND FOOD

MY FORAGING JOURNAL

This small notebook is perfect for foragers to record their finds, making sure that they can find them again in the future, and also to learn from experiences about environmental influences on places where specific plants/mushrooms are likely to grow.

THE FORAGER'S GUIDE TO BOTANY

As your interest, knowledge and skills develop as a forager, you'll notice unfamiliar, sometimes seemingly impenetrable language used by "experts". You could be forgiven for thinking that you need to study for a botany degree to understand it all, but no more.

After reading The Forager's Guide to Botany you'll have a good understanding of the botanical terminology and concepts needed to advance your foraging learning.

FORAGING FOR WILD FOOD IN ENGLAND – SUMMER EDITION

A handy small book highlighting common summertime plants to be found in England, and some general introductory information about foraging.

FORAGING FOR WILD FOOD IN ENGLAND – AUTUMN EDITION

A handy small book highlighting common autumn plants to be found in England, and some general introductory information about foraging.

FORAGING FOR WILD FOOD IN ENGLAND COOKBOOK

A handy small companion to the Foraging for Wild Food in England series, with handy recipes for the common edible plants and fungi found in that series.

ALSO AVAILABLE THROUGH FOUNDFOOD.COM

Since 2010, Found Food has been helping foraging enthusiasts to learn more about their surroundings and how they can best make use of the natural resources all around.

THE FORAGER HELPER

The Forager Helper is a repository of the knowledge that Gavin has built up over the years or foraging, wildcrafting, and studying. At the time of publishing there were over 100 plant, tree, and fungi monographs, videos, recipes, and plant and fungi family descriptions.

Find out more at www.foragerhelper.foundfood.com

SIMPLE BOTANY FOR FORAGERS

This is an online course which this book was designed to accompany. It includes video chapters, quizzes, and downloadable information sheets.

FACE-TO-FACE FORAGING WALKS

You can book face-to-face foraging walks covering Introductions to Foraging, Forage and Feast (which includes a foraging themed picnic), and Forage and Cook (which includes cooking a meal using the things we've foraged along the way), or you can request a custom walk/course.

FORAGING COACHING

If you're looking to become a foraging teacher, or just want to develop your skills and deepen your understanding, a series of coaching calls can help you to achieve that.

Copyright ©2024 Found Food Ltd

All photos by Gavin Ireland.

All rights reserved. No part of this book may be reproduced by any mechanical, photographic, or electronic process, or in the form of a phonographic recording; nor may it be stored in a retrieval system, transmitted, or otherwise copied for public or private use – other than for "fair use" as brief quotations embedded in articles and reviews – without prior written permission of the publisher and FoundFood.com.

The author of this book does not dispense medical advice or prescribe the use of any technique as a form of treatment for physical, emotional, or medical problems without the advice of a physician, either directly or indirectly. The intent of the author is only to provide information of a general nature to help you to learn more about botany, plant identification and usage of those plants. In the event that you use any of the information in this book for yourself or others, the author and publisher assume no responsibility for your actions.

TABLE OF CONTENTS

Introduction 8
  Foraging in England 8
  So why do you want to go foraging? 9

Part 1 - Building the Foundations of Foraging 10
  The power of wild food for nutrition and medicine 10
  Getting to know where you live 12
    Choose a spot to get to know really well 13
    Your foraging journal 14
  Foraging principles 16
    The law 16
    Your responsibility 17
    Awareness of harvesting 18
  Poisonous plants to watch out for 19
  Poison Hemlock (*Conium maculatum*) 20
  Hemlock Water Dropwort (*Oenanthe crocata*) 21
  Foxglove (Digitalis purpurea) 22
  Lords and Ladies (*Arum maculatum*) 23
  Giant Hogweed (Heracleum mantegazzianum) 24
  Dog's Mercury (Mercurialis perennis) 25

Part 2 - Spring Foraging 26
  Wild Garlic (*Allium ursinum*) 28
  Garlic Mustard (*Alliaria petiolata*) 34
  Ground Ivy (*Glechoma hederacea*) 40
  Stinging Nettles (*Urtica dioica*) 46
  Ribwort Plantain (*Plantago lanceolata*) 52
  Cuckoo Flower (*Cardamine pratensis*) 58

Bramble Shoots (*Rubus fruticosus*) 62
Dandelion Flowers (*Taraxacum officinale*) 68
Rosebay Willowherb (*Epilobium angustifolium*) 74
Common Sorrel (*Rumex acetosa*) 78
Scarlet Elf Cups (*Sarcoscypha austriaca*) 82

Next Steps **85**
About the Author **86**

INTRODUCTION

FORAGING IN ENGLAND

England is full of unique and beautiful environments, which sit alongside cultural attractions and its amazing cities and countryside. With rivers, lakes and canals, the many and varied national parks, and areas of outstanding natural beauty, and a wide variety of wild plants, fungi, and animals.

English countryside

England is the centre of the United Kingdom with a temperate climate and environments as diverse as rain forests, cities and towns, craggy windswept highlands, and warm, sheltered lowlands. The clear seas, bright harbours and hidden coves of the coastline give way to busy market towns and the tranquillity of lush green valleys, rolling hills, and shimmering lakes.

As the chill of winter gives way to the warmth of spring, England transforms into a kaleidoscope of colours, scents, and sounds, inviting visitors to experience the beauty and excitement of the region. From the rolling hills of the South to the majestic mountains of the North, city sights and tracts of countryside, nature adorns the landscape with cherry blossoms, daffodils, and playful lambs, creating picturesque scenes straight out of a storybook.

A lot of the edible and medicinal plants and fungi of the UK can be found in many places, what tends to vary is how common and widespread they are, so this guide focusses on the plants and fungi that are common and widespread in England. For example, Rosebay Willowherb (*Chamaenerion angustifolium*) can be found throughout the UK, but nearly every lane and road in England turns bright pink in the spring when Rosebay flowers.

So why do you want to go foraging?

It could be that you're looking at the survival aspect and you want to know that you could survive on wild food if you needed to; it could be that you're looking to reduce your carbon footprint and packaging waste by using more local ingredients in your diet; or maybe you're looking to reduce your food bill by using free ingredients from nature; or you want to introduce some new flavours into your diet which you would otherwise never experience. Maybe for you it's a combination of two or more of those reasons, it doesn't really matter because the principles remain the same. Whatever your reasons it's important to know how to go about it safely, responsibly, and legally.

Part 1 - Building the Foundations of Foraging

The power of wild food for nutrition and medicine

The human "diet" was once seasonal, and highly varied. Given that different food plants have a wide spectrum of micro-nutrients, and that our modern diet consists of much less variety, how much nutrition and culinary medicine are we missing out on?

As far back as records go, there is evidence that we used plants for medicine, and regardless of what type of diet you follow and why, our physiology tells us that we are designed to be omnivorous (meaning our bodies are equipped to deal with meat and plants in our diet), therefore it is a safe assumption that we get a large proportion of our nutrition from the plants that we eat. Indeed, it is possible and is evidenced every day that humans can thrive on a diet of plant-based food alone, whilst the same cannot be said of a solely meat-based diet. Over thousands of years, the human race has developed increasingly efficient methods to produce vast quantities of food crops for consumption, and at the same time we've learned how to make the crops uniform, brightly coloured and sweeter to appeal to modern human cravings. Sometimes all of this advancement has been at the cost of nutrition and goodness.

Of the estimated 400,000 plant species on the planet, approximately 300,000 could be eaten, yet human beings eat around 200 species and of those, 3 species contribute to our plant-sourced protein and calories: maize, rice, and wheat. Given that our habit of eating only a few plant species is a relatively new thing, over the last 200 years or so, how much nutrition and medicine are we missing out on? One might even draw connections between this and the increase in cancers, arthritis, and other life-limiting illnesses over a similar period. That's a bigger question than can be answered in a foraging book but suffice to say that I've never felt better since foraging regularly and I hear the same thing from other foragers too.

This book does not cover the subject of herbalism, that would need a series of books to itself! However, where appropriate I will mention of few of the medicinal properties of the plants we look at in the following sections. Most of our modern medicines are extracts of or synthesised from plants or fungus, so foraging for medicinal plants is also a practice experiencing a revival too.

Getting to know where you live

If we're all so concerned nowadays about reducing our carbon footprints and trying to reverse the environmental damage we cause, why are so many people totally unaware of the food that grows all around them? We can all do our bit by trying to avoid buying produce that has travels hundreds of miles or using public/human powered transport to get to the shops, but we can also look at what's growing right outside our door.

Where you live will have a profound effect on which wild plants grow near you, whether they are thriving or merely surviving, their nutritional values and potentially whether they are safe to consume or not.

From a geographical point of view England is in a temperate climate zone, meaning that we do not experience the extremes of temperatures which you might see in the equatorial or polar zones. However, in England we also have a very wet environment with relatively high levels of rainfall Also, within our temperate zone you'll find differences depending on whether you live in a city, a forest, an agricultural area, on the coast and so on. This small book cannot cover all of those environments, so it is up to you to use some basic principles and really get to know where you live.

The first step is to really observe. Not just make a note that you live in a suburban area of a temperate region. What grows really well where you are? Does a particular type of tree seem to pop up everywhere? Does one type of weed appear in every pavement crack? Does it seem that no matter how much you search you can never find that plant which seems common and widespread everywhere else? This first step of getting to know where you live also becomes your first step to learning about more plants. At the early stages, instead of spending time learning about an interesting plant and searching in vain, choose the plants you see all the time, learn what they are, understand their lifecycle and see if they can be of any use to you.

CHOOSE A SPOT TO GET TO KNOW REALLY WELL

One of the best ways I've found to get to know and to connect with my local area, is to find a safe, accessible spot where I can sit and observe. Sometimes it's only for ten minutes, sometimes for hours, but the key is that it needs to be somewhere that I can keep going back to throughout the year. Your spot can be under a tree, on a park bench, or anywhere you choose where you can peacefully observe nature. Your first choice of spot may not turn out to be the best, so be prepared to find another one. If you have the time, maybe you'll have several spots, but remember you're here to observe and learn as well as to relax and enjoy being outside.

This is where your journal can come in handy, noting what grows and when, describing the weather, how you're feeling, volume of other people and animals and so on. It can also be the place to make a note of whether you'll return there or not, and if not, why?

YOUR FORAGING JOURNAL

First and foremost, my journal acts as an aide-memoire for all of the wonderful things I've seen and would like to be able to find again one day. I've lost track of the number of times over the years I've found myself in the correct season for Porcini mushrooms, for example, but I can't remember where I saw them! Was it local, or while I was away somewhere? If it was local, where exactly was it? Once I started journaling, it saved me a lot of time finding plants, trees, and mushrooms.

Things to consider for your journal:

- Describe where you are and how to get there.
- The closest large geographical feature (e.g., coastline, mountains, forests, lakes etc.)
- What is the soil like? (e.g., sticky, crumbly, thin, etc.)
- What are the levels of rainfall like? How hot and cold does it get?
- List some common trees you can identify – if you don't know their names yet, describe/draw/photograph them.
- List some common plants you can identify – if you don't know their names yet, describe/draw/photograph them.
- List some common fungi you can identify – if you don't know their names yet, describe/draw/photograph them.
- List some common insects you can identify, and the plants you see them on or around – if you don't know their names yet, describe/draw/photograph them.
- List some common animals you can identify, and the plants you see them on or around – if you don't know their names yet, describe/draw/photograph them.
- List some common birds you can identify, and the plants you see them on or around – if you don't know their names yet, describe/draw/photograph them.

- Consider whether the plants and animals you've identified are native, introduced, invasive or even endangered.
- Are there native/first people in the area? Who are they?
- Is there a local history of plant/land usage?
- Where does drinking water come from and where does waste water go?
- Who are your neighbours here?

These can be quite difficult questions to answer sometimes, so consider approaching local people that have been around a long time, local historians, local teachers, gardening and allotment groups, field guides, libraries and museums, park groups/societies, environmental organisations, and local universities/colleges.

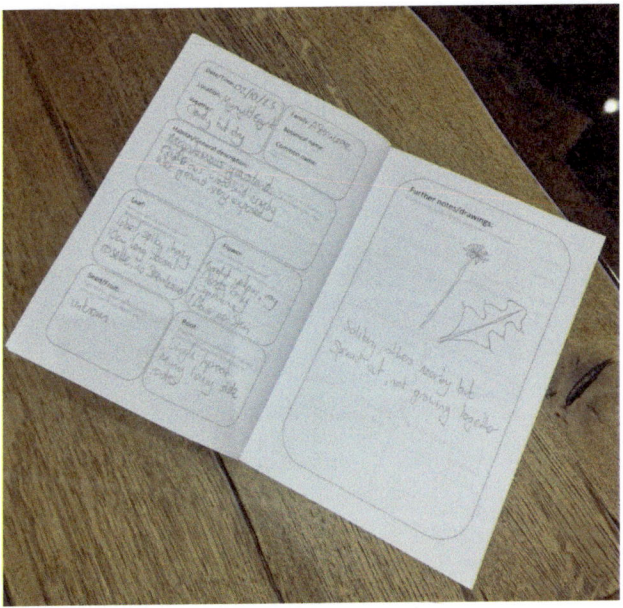

You can find a downloadable, printable version of my template here: https://foundfood.com/wp-content/uploads/2024/01/Journal_download.pdf

Or buy a pre-printed book of journal pages here: https://shop.foundfood.com/products/my-foraging-journal

Foraging principles

Our principles are the high-level rules by which we live our lives. They are self-imposed, not dictated to us, a moral code if you will. We can break other people's rules and still feel OK about ourselves (in some situations), but when we go against our own principles it usually feels pretty bad.

What are foraging principles? Well, to me principles are high-level beliefs and considerations, foraging morals maybe, general non-specific guidelines that you can take with you wherever you are in the world and on your foraging journey.

Blackberry bush

THE LAW

The first thing we need to be mindful of is the law. The overriding principle is this: "Be aware and respectful of the laws and rules relating to foraging where you are." Not knowing what the laws are is not an acceptable excuse to police or to courts.

Within the UK, there are different rules and laws depending on where you are. In England, if you have the right to be there then you can be confident that it's OK foraging leaves, flowers, fruits, seeds, fungus, and bark (responsibly and carefully harvested); However, if you want to collect roots, or do anything else that may cause serious or lasting harm, you need to have the landowner's permission. Contrary to popular belief, just about all land in England is owned by someone, even "common land". You should also be aware of any "protected species" – certain plants are listed as protected because they are endangered, and we don't want them to disappear altogether. Generally, you won't be likely to forage any of those plants, but it is important to be aware of them. Finally, in England we also have bylaws, which are locally enacted laws which may apply restrictions to foraging activity. Now, you'll find lots of advice about the legality of certain rules and regulations on the internet, and from certain experts, but if you ever end up in court, the buck stops with you; so, make sure you're aware of the rules and understand the risks.

YOUR RESPONSIBILITY

As a forager, I take on the responsibility for caring for the environment that I take from. It's not as simple as "only taking what you need", although that's very important. It's not just about "do no harm", which again is important too.

Trampled wild garlic (Allium ursinum)

When I see a patch of wild garlic that has been trampled to mud, stripped of any sign of the plants, and surrounding plants damaged,

I'm not only saddened, disgusted and angry, I'm also thinking how can I fix this? Yes, it's not my fault, and yes I might be fixing it only to have the same thing happen again, but maybe someone will see the cared for and nurtured spot and think twice about doing it again, maybe I can reduce the knock-on damage to the surrounding habitat and make it better for the future.

Likewise, when I see piles of litter in my environment, yes, it's not my fault, yes it's not my job to pick it up, but if everyone thinks like that, the litter will harm the plants and wildlife in my environment and I don't want that.

AWARENESS OF HARVESTING

There are many self-imposed rules out there that foragers will use and share, such as only pick from every tenth plant, or only take 40% of what's available; but I would suggest that a little more care is needed. For example, consider how abundant the plant is locally – some plants are plentiful in some parts and scarce in others, if the plant is scarce where you are maybe consider not taking any at all. Which stage of the growth cycle is the plant in? Would harvesting it now prevent its continued growth cycle? How healthy are these particular plants? Maybe you can help to nurture this area so you can harvest in the future when it's better?

Poisonous plants to watch out for

The majority of plants are safe to handle, and a lot are safe to consume, however there are some that can cause discomfort, sickness and even death. The worst of these are the ones that look a lot like good edible plants. So, as well as learning plant families for identification, it's also worth learning the common dangerous species in isolation too. Here are six common and widespread dangerous plants in England worth knowing:

Poison Hemlock (*Conium maculatum*).

Poison hemlock leaves

From the *Apiaceae* family we mentioned earlier, eating Hemlock usually results in death. It can grow as tall as 15 feet, with a hollow stem that usually has purple splotches on it. One of the things that makes it so dangerous is that it looks just like some kind of wild parsley, especially around the leaves and flowers. It can be difficult to tell the difference between this and cow parsley (*Anthriscus sylvestris*).

HEMLOCK WATER DROPWORT (*OENANTHE CROCATA*).

Hemlock water dropwort leaves

This is another member of the *Apiaceae* family. Again, highly poisonous, usually causing death; and again, so dangerous because the above ground parts look like celery, and the roots look a lot like water parsnip (all also *Apiaceae*).

FOXGLOVE (DIGITALIS PURPUREA)

Foxglove flowers

Foxglove can cause severe sickness and death if you eat it. The toxins in Digitalis can act pretty quickly on the heart and stop it from working. Very common in and near woodland, and very pretty, it has a basal rosette of velvety soft-haired leaves and a tall spike of bell-shaped flowers (usually purple or pink). Sometimes the young leaves are confused with Comfrey and Mullein.

LORDS AND LADIES (*ARUM MACULATUM*)

Arum flower and leaves

This plant has many, many common names so demonstrating the importance of scientific names! Unlike the previous plants, Arum is not strictly speaking poisonous; However, it has microscopic, needle-sharp crystals that can pierce the cell walls of your mucous membranes. For most people that have experienced this, it means the most intense and painful pins and needles in your lips tongue and mouth, along with inflammation and swelling, all of which lasts at least a few hours. That alone is bad enough, but imagine you swallowed it instead of spitting it out? The same reaction in your throat causes swelling that you are unable to breathe and therefore causes death.

Giant Hogweed (Heracleum mantegazzianum).

Giant hogweed leaves

Back to the *Apiaceae* family again, I did say it had lots of dangerous species! Giant hogweed sap can cause photodermatitis, which when exposed to sunlight causes extreme sunburn and blistering. Some people have reported symptoms from merely touching the leaves or stem; However, in most cases, it is from cutting or breaking the plant and coming into contact with the sap. It can't be simply washed off (although you should remove it from your skin to prevent further damage) and can remain active for many years. It's related namesake, Common Hogweed (*Heracleum sphondylium*) is a common and popular edible and can look similar when young. Giant hogweed grows to 20 feet tall, with wide spreading umbels of white flowers. It has thick ridged stems with purple splotches, and unlike common hogweed has shiny, hairless leaves.

Dog's Mercury (Mercurialis perennis)

Dog's mercury leaves and flowers

This can cause vomiting, jaundice, coma, and death from eating it. It is a very common woodland plant, and although it doesn't look much like edible plants, it is so common and widespread that it would be easy to accidentally grab a few stems whilst harvesting wild garlic, nettles, ground ivy etc.

Looking at plant families can seem overwhelming, now I've added a small handful of the toxic plants to look out for too! Sorry about that, but it's important to at least be aware of them until you can confidently identify them. Also, it is a lot to learn, but what can help is to pick a common local plant and get to know it well, before moving onto the next, rather than trying to learn about them all and getting stuck.

PART 2 - SPRING FORAGING

I'm often asked, "which is the best month for foraging?", or "Which is the best season?" and frustratingly my answer is usually something along the lines of "they're all great, it just depends on what you're looking for".

I guess when it comes down to it though, Spring has the edge because the cold of Winter is fading, and all the new growth is coming through bright and fresh.

Spring means greens for salads and for cooking, herbs starting to come through for flavouring, buds are plumping up ready for picking, some winter roots will still be available, and the promise of spring mushrooms is in my mind.

Remembering that this is supposed to be a getting started guide, I've selected some common, easy to recognise and easy to use spring plants to get you started. Each plant includes as much information as I thought you might need (or could stand at this early stage).

WILD GARLIC (*ALLIUM URSINUM*)

Whilst there are various plants known collectively as "wild garlics", such as three-cornered leek, few-flowered leek, and crow garlic, this article is about the white star flowered perennial that pops up for a few weeks in spring every year.

It's one of the simplest wild plants to identify (by virtue of the fact that it reeks of garlic) and really easy to use, so it's no wonder that new and experienced foragers alike go mad for this weed each spring.

Wild Garlic flowers

KEY INFORMATION

Common names: Wild garlic, bear garlic, bear leek, ramsons, ramps, wild cowleek, cowlick, broad-leaved garlic, wood garlic, and buckrams.

Botanical name: *Allium ursinum*

Family: *Amaryllidaceae*

Parts used: Leaves, flowers, flower buds, bulbs, seeds.

Distribution

Native to Europe and Asia, found in most regions in the British Isles.

Habitat

Wild garlic likes slightly acidic, damp soils in deciduous woods, and can often be found on riversides and valleys.

It is said that wild garlic is an indicator of ancient woods, and it can often be found in the same spot as bluebells.

How to identify wild garlic

Wild garlic is a bulbous perennial flowering plant, related to onions and garlic.

It spends most of the year as a bulb underground, only emerging to flower and leaf from February/March onwards. This allows it to make the most of the sunlight on the forest floor before the canopy becomes too dense and blocks the sunlight out. Millions of bulbs may exist in one spot, causing the white, starry carpets and strong garlic smell we so keenly associate with this flower. Wild garlic attracts the attention of plenty of pollinating insects, including hoverflies, butterflies, and longhorn beetles.

Each plant has a single narrow bulb under the ground. Unlike cultivated garlic bulbs, these are especially thin and not easily broken into separate sections.

The leaves are green, entire, and elliptical. Often described as "strap-like" shaped. Usually up to 25cm long and 7cm wide with a petiole up to 20cm long. Depending on the growth stage and conditions there can be from one to six leaves per plant. They emit a strong garlic scent when bruised.

Wild Garlic leaves

The inflorescence is an umbel of six to 20 white, star-shaped flowers. Each flower has six white tepals, about 16-20mm diameter. The stamens are shorter than the petals.

Wild Garlic flowers

Food

The leaves can be eaten raw or cooked. Raw, they tend to have a strong garlic flavour that works really well in salads, pesto and other in-cooked dishes. On cooking, the garlic flavour fades considerably. The weaker flavour is desirable sometimes, but if you want to maintain the strong garlic flavour in a hot dish, I recommend stirring into the dish just before serving.

The flowers also can be eaten raw or cooked. These tend to be a little stronger flavoured than the leaves and make an attractive addition to a cold dish. You can still eat the flowers as the seed pods begin to form, but the flavour gets stronger as the seeds mature.

The bulbs also can be eaten raw or cooked, if you're the type of person that likes to eat raw garlic. The strongest garlic flavour of the plant, but a little small and fiddly. If you're going to cook with wild garlic, this is the part to use.

Medicine

Wild garlic has most of the health benefits associated with cultivated garlic (*Allium sativum*), although it is not a strong so makes a good addition to the diet, promoting general health.

Known hazards

No hazards known for human consumption, but there have been reports of dogs being poisoned after eating large amounts of wild garlic.

Harvesting

Depending on where you are and the weather conditions, the leaves usually start appearing from early February and can be harvested straight away.

Flowering usually begins a few weeks later.

Bulbs are best gathered during the dormant season, from early summer to winter. Of course, making sure you have permission to dig up the bulbs.

Potential lookalikes

The biggest issue with dangerous lookalikes when foraging wild garlic, as with other plants, is accidentally grabbing other plants as you try to grab big fistfuls of garlic leaves. There is nothing else that looks like wild garlic and smells of garlic.

Lily of the valley (*Convallaria majalis*), autumn crocus (*Colchicum autumnale*), *Arum maculatum*, and helebore (*Veratrum album*), all have similar looking leaves to one degree or another, but none have the distinct garlic smell when you crush their leaves.

Top tip: Make sure your hands don't already smell of garlic before checking another plant!

Mythology and symbolism

In Ireland, the bulbs of wild garlic were sown into the thatch of cottages for good luck and to keep fairies out.

Wild garlic isn't welcome everywhere, and in several places in the UK you can hear stories of kids being paid to stamp on or pull up plants to stop cows from eating it. It was believed that the garlic flavour would ruin the milk and butter. That sounds to me like a bit of marketing is needed to sell the naturally flavoured wild garlic butter and cheese!

In ancient Greece, Dioscorides believed that was an effective cure for snake bites.

A. Allium ursinum L. Bären-Lauch.
B. Allium nigrum L. Schwarzer Lauch.

Garlic Mustard (*Alliaria petiolata*)

For such a widespread and versatile food plant, this invasive weed is distinctly lacking in folklore and mythology. Maybe we should make up some new stories for it.

Now I know that this will upset some "purists", but I frequently refer to this as one of our wild garlics. I know it's not a member of the *Amaryllidaceae* family as wild garlics are, but it's a wild plant and it smells and tastes of garlic, so there! Being a more of a mustard than a garlic means that the leaves can sometimes have a bitter aftertaste (particularly older leaves), but it is also available almost all year round so much easier to find than the true garlics.

Key information

Common names: Garlic root, hedge garlic, jack-by-the-hedge, jack-in-the-bush, penny hedge, sauce alone, poor man's mustard.

Botanical name: *Alliaria petiolata*

Family: *Brassicaceae*

Parts used: Young leaves, flowers, seeds, stems and roots.

Distribution

Native to most of Europe, southwards to north Africa, eastwards to west Asia and the Himalayas, and northwards to northern Scandinavia. Introduced to North America where it has spread across the continent and is considered an invasive weed.

Habitat

As suggested by some of the common names, it likes to grow in hedgerows, on the edges of woodlands and woodland clearings.

How to identify garlic mustard

It is an herbaceous biennial plant growing from a deeply growing, thin, white taproot that smells like horseradish. In the first year, plants appear as a rosette of green leaves close to the ground; these rosettes remain green through the winter and develop into mature flowering plants the following spring. Second year plants grow from 30–100 cm tall and rarely to 130 cm.

The leaves are stalked, triangular to heart-shaped, 10–15 cm long (of which about half being the petiole) and 5–9 cm broad, with a coarsely toothed margin. The leaves smell strongly of garlic when crushed.

The flowers are produced in spring and summer in button-like clusters. Each small flower has four white petals 4–8 mm long and 2–3 mm broad, arranged in a cross shape as is common for Brassicaceae plants.

The fruit is an erect, slender, four-sided pod 4–5.5 cm long, called a "silique", green maturing pale grey-brown, containing two rows of small shiny black seeds which are released when the pod splits open.

A single plant can produce hundreds of seeds, which scatter as much as several meters from the parent plant. The mature seeds are black, oval and 2.5 to 3 mm long.

Food

The young leaves can be raw or cooked as a herb or flavouring in cooked foods. They have a mild garlic and mustard flavour; the leaves are also believed to strengthen the digestive system. They can be finely chopped and added to salads. The leaves are available very early in the year and provide a very acceptable flavouring for salads in the winter. The leaves can have quite a bitter aftertaste which can be removed with gentle heat – for example being stirred into mash or risotto.

Flowers and young seed pods – raw. A mild, garlic-like flavour. When green, the seeds taste like a sweet garlic, as they mature to black, the taste becomes more pungent, like mustard; Good for clearing the sinuses!

Medicine

Garlic mustard has been little used in western herbal medicine. The leaves have been taken internally to promote sweating and to treat bronchitis, asthma, and eczema. Externally, they have been used as an antiseptic poultice on ulcers etc and are effective in relieving the itching caused by bites and stings.

Known hazards

No known hazards.

Harvesting

The leaves and stems are usually harvested before the plant comes into flower and they can be dried for later use if necessary. The leaves can survive winter and can even be found under snow – they contain natural anti-freeze which protects them from frost damage.

The flowers can be eaten any time they're visible.

The seed pods can be harvested when green in late summer for a sweet mustard-garlic snack. They can also be harvested later in the year once the pods have turned brown, for a stronger mustard seed flavour.

Potential lookalikes

Violet species and ground ivy have similar leaf shapes when viewed separately from garlic mustard but crushing the leaves to release the garlic smell soon identifies this plant.

There are no poisonous lookalikes that I'm aware of.

Other uses

A yellow dye can be made from garlic mustard.

Garlic mustard and wildlife

Many insects are associated with garlic mustard in Europe including leaf beetles, the garden carpet moth, and the orange tip butterfly.

Apparently, in North America it is considered to be of no benefit to wildlife and is toxic to the larvae of certain rare butterfly species.

LÖKTRAV, ALLIARIA OFFICINALIS ANDRZ.

Ground Ivy (*Glechoma hederacea*)

The taste of Ground Ivy raw is so pungent that it is difficult for most people to chew an entire leaf; However, that flavour mellows considerably on cooking, and so makes an excellent addition for stock, sauces, and gravies.

Depending on the local conditions, ground ivy can grow entirely along the floor, or as an upright, two to three feet tall herb.

Key information

Common names: Ground ivy, alehoof, creeping Charlie, field balm, gill over the ground, runaway robin, tunhoof.

Botanical name: *Glechoma hederacea*

Family: *Lamiaceae*

Parts used: Leaves, flowers, and stems.

Distribution

Most of Europe, including Britain, northern and western Asia to Japan.

Habitat

Ground ivy likes damp waste ground, hedgerows, and woodland margins.

How to identify Ground Ivy

Glechoma hederacea is an aromatic, perennial, evergreen creeper of the mint family, *Lamiaceae*. It thrives in moist shaded areas, but also tolerates sun very well. It is a common plant in grasslands and wooded areas or wasteland. It also thrives in lawns and around buildings since it survives mowing. It spreads by seed or by putting down roots at the leaf junctions where it is laying across the ground.

The bright green round to reniform (kidney or fan shaped), crenate (with round toothed edges) opposed leaves 2–3 cm diameter, on 3–6 cm long petioles. Usually more round toward the end of a stem and more heart-shaped near the base.

Ground Ivy leaf

The stems, like other mints, have a square cross-section and soft hairs.

The tiny flowers are bilaterally symmetrical, funnel shaped, blue or bluish violet to lavender with white and dark purple spots on the lower lip, believed to be designed to attract pollinating insects. The flowers grow in opposed clusters of two or three flowers in the leaf axils on the upper part of the stem or near the tip. It usually flowers from March to June, then again in the Autumn.

Ground Ivy flower

FOOD

Young leaves, stems and flowers can be chopped into a salad and eaten raw. However, most people find the taste to be far too pungent for eating raw, maybe in very small amounts, chopped finely would be OK. With such a strong flavour, they make an excellent addition to stocks, stews and soups and the flavour tends to soften with cooking. A spring herb tea combining ground ivy with verbena leaves has been popular in the past.

Ground ivy was used widely by the Saxons in beer brewing where it clarifies, preserves, and bitters the ale. Hence the common names "alehoof" and "tunhoof".

Ground ivy has also been used as a substitute for rennet in the cheese making process.

MEDICINE

Ground ivy was traditionally considered a safe and effective herb that is used to treat many problems involving the mucous membranes of the ear, nose, throat, and digestive system. It was given to children to clear lingering catarrh and to treat chronic conditions such as glue ear and sinusitis. Applied externally, the expressed juice is said to speed the healing of bruises and black eyes.

KNOWN HAZARDS

Generally, moderate amounts with food are OK, but apparently it is best avoided if you suffer from epilepsy or kidney disease.

Avoid during pregnancy as it was used as an abortifacient in the past.

HARVESTING

The leaves can start to appear as early as February/March, and if you're going to use the leaves it's best to get them while they're still young and fresh. Traditional advice was that they are best harvested in May whilst still fresh and are dried for later use.

POTENTIAL LOOKALIKES

Apparently, *Glechoma* is sometimes confused with common mallow (*Malva neglecta*), which also has round, lobed leaves; but mallow leaves are attached to the stem at the back of a rounded leaf, where ground ivy has square stems and leaves which are attached in the centre of the leaf, more prominent rounded lobes on their edges, attach to the stems in an opposite arrangement, and have a hairy upper surface.

That said, in my experience ground ivy and common mallow aren't easily confused; Much more likely is possible confusion between ground ivy and garlic mustard (*Alliaria petiolata*) which has a very similar leaf shape and certainly for beginners can have very similar looking leaves.

Above all, ground ivy emits a distinctive odour when damaged, being a member of the mint family.

Mythology and symbolism

Because it forms long, leafy, flowering, trailing stems, it is no surprise that is was often woven into garlands. Such garlands were used to protect cattle (despite it being poisonous to cattle!) and apparently the first milk was passed through a wreath of ground ivy to protect it in some parts of the world.

Stinging Nettles (*Urtica dioica*)

Forget your quinoa, your goji berries, your avocados, and any other "super-foods" that clock up millions of miles to get to your local supermarket or health food shop. Stinging nettles are our own native superfood. Every bit as nutritious as the exotic sounding imports (if not more!) and much better for the planet as just about everyone can find some growing a short walk away.

Key information

Common names: Burn hazel, burn nettle, burn weed, common nettle.

Botanical name: *Urtica dioica*

Family: *Urticaceae*

Parts used: Young leaves, flowers, seeds.

Distribution

Stinging nettles are native to Europe, northern Africa, and North America; and have been introduced widely elsewhere.

Habitat

They can usually be found on waste ground, disturbed areas, ditches, marshes, in hedgerows and woods. They prefer a rich soil but tend to avoid acid soils.

Patches of bright, healthy nettles are said to be an indicator of fertile ground, and possibly an indicator of previous human occupation.

How to identify stinging nettles

It is a quick-growing, herbaceous perennial which can reach a height of 1.2 metres very quickly.

There are actually six sub-species of stinging nettles, but for food purposes we treat them all the same.

Stinting nettles have soft green leaves from 3 to 15cm long, with serrate edges. The leaves grow in opposite pairs on an erect stem (which has a square cross-section). The leaves and stems are very hairy and most sub-species also have stinging hairs which inject chemicals into the skin causing pain and irritation.

Nettles have tiny green flowers which usually grow in dense bunches. Later the female plant has dense bunches of green seeds, turning brown when they're ripe.

Food

The young leaves can be eaten raw (with care, crush the leaves thoroughly to break the stings!), boiled as a spinach replacement, and they also make excellent crisps.

Nettles are high in minerals, vitamins, and other nutrients such as calcium, manganese, iron, potassium, copper, magnesium, zinc, phosphorus, flavonoids, ascorbic acid, glucosamine, beta-carotene, vitamin A, B, C and K, fibre, and protein; In fact, nettles are so high in protein that they could be a very valuable addition to a meat-free diet.

MEDICINE

Nettles have a long history of use in the home as a herbal remedy and nutritious addition to the diet. A tea made from the leaves has traditionally been used as a cleansing tonic and blood purifier, so the plant is often used in the treatment of hay fever, arthritis, anaemia etc.

KNOWN HAZARDS

The leaves and stems of the plants have stinging hairs which cause irritation to the skin. The stinging action is neutralised by cooking, thoroughly drying, or crushing the leaves.

Older leaves can build up gritty particles inside which can irritate the kidneys, so best to only consume younger leaves.

It is generally advised to avoid nettle consumption during pregnancy.

HARVESTING

Usually in leaf from March and flowering from May to October.

Gather only the top four to eight leaves from bright and healthy-looking plants. Stinging nettles are quick-growing weeds, so if you only have older, or sickly-looking ones, cut them back and return a week later to gather the fresh new leaves.

You can gather nettle seeds from the female plant from late August into September.

POTENTIAL LOOKALIKES

White deadnettle (*Lamium album*) can look very similar and regularly grows in the same places. Can be identified by its white flowers and lack of stings. White deadnettle is also a good edible, so there's no risk if you do get it wrong.

Mythology and Symbolism

Being very common, the stinging nettle has much lore and myth surrounding it; here are some of the more common ones:

The name "Nettle" is said to have come from the Anglo-Saxon word for needle, probably referring to its stinging needles (hairs), or possibly referring to its value as a thread (seems less likely).

In Irish mythology, when the children of Lir (sea god) returned from hundreds of years in exile, they found their home overgrown with nettles; as did Oisin on returning to his great hall. Unsurprising when nettles are so commonly found in wasteland and abandoned places.

Dreaming of gathering nettles is said to mean that someone likes you, or that your marriage will be a happy one; Whereas dreaming of being stung means something bad is coming.

In Germany and Wales, folk songs associate nettles with love and fertility.

Across the British Isles, many stories exist concerning the origin of nettles, including that they mark the spots where Satan and his fallen angels fell to earth, that they grow from dead men's bodies or from the spilling of innocents' blood, and that they grow from human urine (though they do prefer nitrogen rich soil, so there may be some truth in that one!).

Stinging Nettles and Wildlife

Stinging nettles support more than 40 kinds of insects in the UK. As well as being a food for them, the nettles' stings provide a protective barrier against grazing animals. Over-wintering insects such as aphids provide food for early ladybirds and small birds such as blue tits. Other insect eaters such as hedgehogs, shrews, frogs, and toads are also drawn to nettles for their insects. Also, moths and butterflies value nettles for laying their eggs somewhere safe and which will provide valuable food for their larvae. Small tortoiseshell and peacock butterfly larvae are commonly found on nettles.

178. Urtica dioica L. — Große Brennnessel.

Ribwort Plantain (*Plantago lanceolata*)

There are two common types of plantain herbs in the UK, and three less common. We're going to focus on Ribwort Plantain here, but everything written here will apply to Broadleaf plantain (the other common one), Hoary Plantain, Buck's Horn Plantain and Sea Plantain too.

When we were children, we used to play with the flower stems by wrapping them around our fingers and pulling sharply, which sent the flower head shooting off (usually at someone nearby!).

Key information

Common names: English plantain, narrowleaf plantain, ribleaf.

Botanical name: *Plantago lanceolata*

Family: *Plantaginaceae*

Parts used: Flowers, stems, and leaves.

Distribution

Plantains are native in Europe, northern and central Asia, and introduced in north America.

Habitat

Plantain can live anywhere from very dry meadows to places as wet as a rain forest, but it does best in open and disturbed areas. It is therefore common near roadsides where other plants struggle; it grows tall if it can (I've found a flower stalk about 1m tall), but in frequently mowed areas grows flat instead. Historically, the plant has thrived in areas where cattle graze and turn up the earth with their hooves.

How to identify Plantain

Plantain is a very common temperate perennial weed that forms a basal leaf rosette, with leafless, silky, hairy flower stems.

The basal leaves are lanceolate spreading or erect with 3-5 strong parallel veins narrowing to a short petiole.

The flowers have a deeply furrowed stalk, ending in an ovoid inflorescence of many small flowers each with a pointed bract. Each flower is approximately 4mm (calyx green, corolla brownish), with four bent back lobes with brown midribs, long white stamens, but you need to zoom right in to see all of that detail.

Plantain seed head

Each of the tiny flowers can produce up to two seeds.

FOOD

Young leaves can be eaten raw or cooked. They can be bitter and whilst the fibrous strands are best removed prior to eating, it's not entirely essential. The very young leaves are somewhat better and are less fibrous. At all ages, the leaves have a good mushroom flavour.

The seeds can be ground into a powder and added to flours when making bread, cakes or whatever. However, that is really fiddly given their tiny size.

The leaves and seed heads taste of mushroom and can be boiled up to make a nice mushroom stock. Like the young leaves, the flower heads and seed heads can be eaten raw.

Personally, I Love munching on the raw leaves and seed heads for the mushroom flavour.

MEDICINE

Plantains are known to be an effective treatment for cuts. They help to slow bleeding, encourage the repair of damaged tissue and are antibacterial. They also provide effective relief from nettle stings. The most common folk usage is as a "spit poultice". To make a spit poultice, chew on a few leaves until they're nice and chewed up, then apply to the affected area.

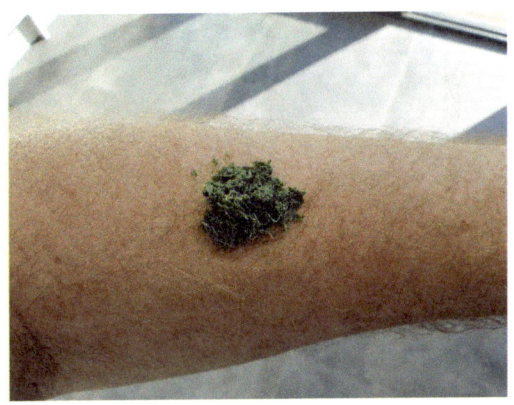

Plantain spit poultice

KNOWN HAZARDS

Plantain has been implicated in seasonal hay fever. Only a hazard if you suffer from hay fever.

HARVESTING

The leaves come up from around march but can be hard to spot when they're young. They tend to hide in grass where they're the same colour.

Flowers start to bloom from April right through to August, and the seeds ripen from June to September.

POTENTIAL LOOKALIKES

Other members of the plantain family are potential lookalikes, but they are all safe and have the same uses.

PLANTAIN AND WILDLIFE

Songbirds are known to eat the seeds and rabbits like eating the leaves.

Many moths and butterflies lay their eggs on Plantain and the larvae eat it when they hatch.

MYTHOLOGY AND SYMBOLISM

Across the British Isles, a game where children would try to knock the flower heads off each other's stalks was common (similar to the game of conkers) and known by many different names, such as 'fighting cocks', 'giants', 'cocks and hens' and 'knights'.

An Irish legend told of a beetle that cured itself by eating a plantain leaf, after being poisoned by the devil's beetle.

In Christian tradition, the 5 ribs of the leaf represent the 5 wounds that Christ received at his crucifixion.

Cuckoo Flower (*Cardamine pratensis*)

In meadows (where the name part "pratensis" comes from), when cuckoo flowers open, the white/pink flowers alongside the bright yellow dandelions, and against the lush green background look beautiful. Their delicate pretty nature belies the powerful punch that they impact on your taste buds!

Key information

Common names: Lady's smock, mayflower, milkmaids.

Botanical name: *Cardamine pratensis*

Family: *Brassicaceae*

Parts used: Flowers, stems, seed pods, and leaves.

Distribution

It is a perennial herb native throughout most of Europe, North America and western Asia.

Habitat

Moist, slightly shady places in meadows and by streams, usually in acid soils. Sometimes on grassy road verges too.

How to identify Cuckoo Flowers

Cardamine pratensis is a herbaceous, hairless, perennial plant growing to 60 cm tall in meadows and grasslands.

The pinnate leaves are 5–12 cm long with 3–15 leaflets, each leaflet about 1 cm long.

The flowers are produced on a spike 10–30 cm long, each flower 1–2 cm in diameter with four very pale violet-pink (rarely white) petals.

Cardamine pratensis flowers

Food

The leaves and young shoots can be eaten raw or cooked. They are rich in vitamins and minerals, especially vitamin C, but with a bitter and pungent flavour like mustard or watercress.

The flowers and flower buds can be eaten raw and have a pungent cress-like flavour. The white flowers are very attractive, they make a pleasant nibble and also add a delicious flavour to salads.

Medicine

Cuckoo flowers are rarely used in herbal medicine, but their pungent, mustard-like flavour can be used to promote digestion for people with a slow digestive transit.

Known hazards

None known.

Harvesting

The leaves come up from around February but can be hard to spot when they're young. They tend to hide in grass where they're the same colour.

Flowers start to bloom from April through to early June.

Potential lookalikes

Before flowering the leaves look similar to the other Cardamines or cress family members but these are all edible too.

Cuckoo flower and wildlife

It is a food plant for the orange tip butterfly (*Anthocharis cardamines*).

Mythology and symbolism

In folklore it was said to be sacred to the fairies, and so was unlucky if brought indoors.

BRAMBLE SHOOTS (*RUBUS FRUTICOSUS*)

In other parts of the world, bramble is used to mean any prickly shrub. Here in the UK we use it to mean the blackberry bush, *Rubus fruticosus*. That isn't where the complication ends though, *Rubus fruticosus* (or *Rubus fruticosus* agg.) is in fact a grouping of over 375 closely related microspecies of plants! The good news is that they're all edible and we can treat them all in the same way.

KEY INFORMATION

Common names: Bramble, blackberry bush, shrubby blackberry.

Botanical name: *Rubus fruticosus*

Family: *Roseacea*

Parts used: Flowers, fruit, stems, and leaves.

Distribution

Rubus Fruticosus is mostly limited to Western Europe and Western Scandanavia, however the closely related blackberry species are to be found across Europe, north-western Africa, western and central Asia and north and south America.

Habitat

There aren't many habitats that Bramble doesn't like. Hedgerows, woodland, meadows, especially common on waste ground.

How to identify Bramble

Bramble is a fast growing and spreading deciduous shrub, growing up to 3m by 3m and spreading quickly to overtake wasteland, scrub and un-tended gardens. It can grow taller if supported by other plants, or its own bushiness, and can grow much longer when trailing along the ground.

The stem has a woody core and can grow up to 2cm thick. Usually covered in sharp, curved prickles. Sometimes the stem has a star-shaped cross section. In the first year the stem grows quickly producing many leaves but no flowers. In the second year the main stem doesn't grow any longer but it produces flowering side stems.

The leaves are large, green, palmately compound with five or seven leaflets. The flowering stems' leaves are smaller, with three or five leaflets.

The flowers are produced in late spring and early summer on short racemes on the tips of the flowering stems. Each flower is about 2–3 cm in diameter, with five white or pale pink petals. Bramble does not flower in the first year.

The fruit, or drupelets grow in bunches around a central "core" and together they form an aggregate fruit, or what we call the blackberry. They appear and ripen to nearly black in the autumn after pollination.

Ripe blackberry fruit

Food

The fruit Can be eaten raw or cooked and there can't be many people that haven't tried it. They fruit can range from sour and strong flavoured to sweet and subtly flavoured depending on variety and how ripe they are. The fruit is also made into syrups, jams, and other preserves, and wine.

The leaves are one of my favourite walking/foraging snacks. When the leaf buds are just opened, but the leaves are not yet spread out, pick off a small bunch and eat. You need to chew them at the back of your mouth until your mouth juices start flowing (they are quite drying at first), then you get the most amazing, complex, savoury flavour comes through. The opened, but still young leaves can be made into a refreshing tea, and the dried leaves are often used in herbal tea blends.

The root can be eaten cooked, but it needs a lot of boiling. Not something I've been tempted to try yet.

The very young shoots can be harvested early in the spring as they emerge from the ground, peeled and eaten raw in salads. You can also wait until they're 5-8mm in diameter, slice into 2-3mm slices and pickle or candy the shoots to make nice star-shaped snacks (some stems have a star-shaped cross section).

Medicine

A decoction of the leaves can be used as a gargle to treat sore throats, mouth ulcers, gum inflammation and also makes a good general mouthwash. Large quantities of the leaves can have a laxative effect.

Known hazards

Apart from the nasty prickles, none known but some people have has stomach upset from eating too many sour (under-ripe) berries.

Harvesting

The leaves are usually out from early spring and you can find those tasty leaf buds most of the year if you look hard enough. The fruit can be picked from August to October.

Potential lookalikes

As mentioned above, there are hundreds of micro species of *R. fruticosus* so you may find a little variation in looks, but they are all edible.

Mythology and symbolism

In the UK it's traditional not to pick blackberries after Old Michaelmas day (11 October) as the Devil will have fouled on them. In Ireland a similar story tells of the Pooka urinating on the berries at Halloween. Generally the fruit is past its best then anyway.

According to some stories, the dark purple colour of the fruit juice represents Christ's blood from the crown of bramble thorns he was made to wear. However, there are just as many stories claiming the thorns to have been other plants such as hawthorn or euphorbia.

Other superstition about bramble includes that stains from the fruit won't come out of clothes with the fruiting season is still on; hair is more likely to fall out during blackberry season, if a girl's dress gets caught by bramble prickles whilst walking with her boyfriend, he will be faithful; and a good blackberry season means a good herring season. In Christian tradition, the 5 ribs of the leaf represent the 5 wounds that Christ received at his crucifixion.

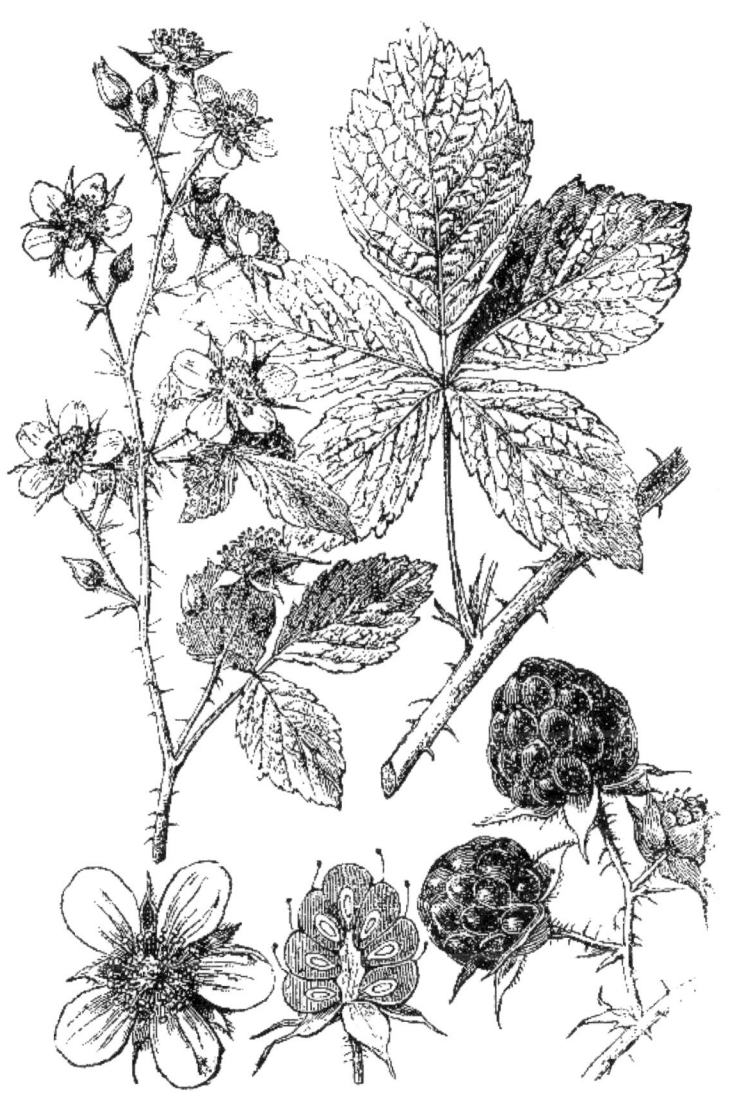

Dandelion Flowers (*Taraxacum officinale*)

This ubiquitous weed, much hated by gardeners has so many uses and actually looks very pretty. Who wants a perfectly manicured lawn anyway?

Key information

Common names: Blowball, cankerwort, dandelion clock, faceclock, Irish daisy, Lion's tooth, milk-witch, monks-head, pee-a-bed, priest's-crown, puff-ball, swine's snout, wet-a-bed, white endive, wild endive, yellow-gowan.

Botanical name: *Taraxacum officinale*

Family: *Asteraceae*

Parts used: Roots, leaves, flower buds, flowers.

Distribution

Dandelions can be found in most temperate regions of the northern hemisphere and is becoming more common in the southern hemisphere too.

Habitat

It is very common on lawns, roadsides, disturbed banks, riversides, meadows and just about anywhere with moist soil.

How to identify Dandelion

Dandelion is a fast growing, herbaceous perennial which typically grows from an unbranched taproot producing a basal rosette of leaves and a single, leafless flower stem, typically up to 40cm tall.

Please note that there are currently over 200 sub-species of dandelion identified, so there will be some variation from the descriptions given here, however all dandelions can be used in the same way so there's no need to get hung up about identifying the exact sub-species.

The flower stem can be up to 40cm tall (occasionally taller), green (sometimes with a purple tinge), circular cross section and hollow. They exude a bitter milky latex when cut. The stems can be hairless or occasionally covered in short hairs.

The leaves are usually up to 40cm long and 8cm wide (occasionally larger) with bases that narrow to the petiole. Leaf margins are usually lobed and tooth-like. The central mid-rib of the leaf and the petiole have the same bitter milky latex as the flower stem.

The flowers are composite, made up of 40 to 100 bright yellow florets and has green sepals.

The fruit, called cypselae, are silver-grey, 2-3mm long, and have 4 to 12 ribs. Each fruit is attached to a silky pappi which catches the wind and helps to distribute the seeds widely.

Dandelion seed head (or "clock")

Food

The leaves can be eaten raw or cooked. When used raw, they can be quite bitter, slightly less so in the winter. To remove the bitterness, strip the leaf material off each side of the central mid-rib and discard the mid-rib. Tender young leaves are considerably less bitter than older leaves. Highly nutritious food, 100g of the raw leaves contain about 2.7g. protein, 9.2g. carbohydrate, 187mg Calcium, 66mg phosphorus, 3.1mg iron, 76mg sodium, 397mg potassium, 36mg magnesium, 14000iu vitamin A, 0.19mg vitamin B1, 0.26mg vitamin B2, 35mg vitamin C.

The root can be eaten raw or cooked. They have a bitter, turnip-like flavour when eaten raw. The roots of 2 year old plants are harvested in the autumn, dried and roasted to make a very good caffeine-free coffee substitute. Also a key component in the carbonated drink "Dandelion and Burdock".

The flowers can be eaten raw or cooked. A slightly bitter flavour on the whole, but sometimes you can bite the middle part out of the flower and taste the honey-like nectar in there. The unopened flower buds can be used in fritters and they can also be preserved in vinegar and used like capers. A sweet tea can also be made from the flowers. The flowers can also be used to make wine and to flavour brandy, and to make a jam.

Medicine

Dandelion is a very commonly used herbal remedy. It is especially effective and valuable as a diuretic because it contains high levels of potassium salts and therefore can replace the potassium that is lost from the body, which is a common problem when diuretics are used. The latex contained in the plant sap can be used to remove corns, warts and verrucae – I can vouch for the efficacy of this, although it does take longer than conventional medicine treatments, but it is natural and free!

Known hazards

None known, although some people have experienced allergies to the Asteraceae family. The latex liquid also has the potential to cause dermatitis.

Harvesting

The leaves are usually harvested in the spring and can be dried for use later. The roots are harvested in the autumn when 2 years old.

Potential lookalikes

Hawkbits (*Leontodon spp.*), Hawkweeds (*Hieracium spp.*), Cat's ear (*Hypochaeris radicata*), and Sow thistle (*Sonchus spp.*) are the most likely to be mistaken for dandelion as the flowers are also bright yellow and composite, like dandelions, and like dandelions both can have toothed leaves in a basal rosette. However, neither of them has a hollow flower stem, they both have branching flower stems with multiple flowers, and Sow thistles have leaves growing up the stems, whereas dandelion do not. Also, none of the lookalikes are toxic so it wouldn't be a terrible mistake to make.

Mythology and symbolism

The one that sticks in my mind most clearly is being told "Don't pick dandelions or you'll wet the bed". Clearly that has got a little mixed up over the years and maybe it started out as "Don't eat dandelions or you'll wet the bed".

In some cultures, dreaming of dandelions is said to be an indication of poor fortune to come.

In springtime, closed dandelion flowers predict rain, fluffy flower heads indicate good weather, and limp flower heads suggest poor weather.

In Greek mythology, before Theseus goes to slay the minotaur, Hecate feeds him a potion which includes dandelion to make him stronger.

Rosebay Willowherb (*Epilobium angustifolium*)

When spring comes around, the countryside turns bright pink from the flowers of Rosebay willowherb.

KEY INFORMATION

Common names: Willowherb, fireweed, great willowherb, bombweed, St. Anthony's laurel.

Botanical name: *Epilobium angustifolium*

Family: *Onagraceae*

Parts used: Flowers, stems, and leaves.

Distribution

Willowherbs are common across almost all of the northern hemisphere.

Habitat

Rocky ground, waste areas, woodland edges and gardens. Rosebay Willowherb is often abundant in wet calcareous to slightly acidic soils in open fields, pastures, and particularly burned-over lands. It is a pioneer species that quickly colonizes open areas with little competition, such as the sites of forest fires and forest clearings. Plants grow and flower as long as there is open space and plenty of light.

How to identify Rosebay Willowherb

Rosebay willowherb is a very common temperate herbaceous perennial weed with scattered alternate leaves. They grow up to 2.5 metres high and usually in large colonies.

The leaves are spirally arranged on the stem, narrow and have a central vein.

The flowers form at the tip of the plant in a terminal raceme, in which the flowers open from the bottom first, with the uppermost flowers opening last. They are bright pink with 4 petals and 4 pink sepals too.

Food

Young shoots can be eaten raw or cooked and are a good source of vitamins A and C, but quickly become too fibrous to eat as they age.

Older stems can be split apart to get to the edible raw pith.

The flowers are edible and can be used to make a sparkling country wine similar to elderflower champagne.

The leaves can be fermented and dried to make a very strong tea, sometimes known as Ivan-chai or Koporsky tea.

Personally, I like to pickle the young shoots as a delicious pickled snack.

Medicine

Whilst not widely used by herbalists, Rosebay Willowherb is used for home remedies for diarrhoea, IBS, prostate issues and mouth ulcers.

Known hazards

None known.

Harvesting

The young shoots are best picked in early spring before they reach 15cm tall. The leaves for tea-making are best collected before the plant flowers. Flowering usually starts from June and can run through to September.

Potential lookalikes

Other willowherbs look superficially similar, but the flowers and height of Rosebay Willowherb are quite distinctive.

Rosebay Willowherb and wildlife

Moths lay their eggs on Rosebay Willowherb and the larvae eat it when they hatch.

Mythology and symbolism

Fireweed is the floral emblem of Yukon.

Rudyard Kipling wrote "The fire-weed glows in the centre of the drive ways".

As the first plant to colonise waste ground, fireweed is often mentioned in postwar British literature.

Epilobium angustifolium

COMMON SORREL (*RUMEX ACETOSA*)

For a very ordinary green leaf, often overlooked amongst the grass, sorrel packs quite a flavour punch; Often compared to lemon, or as I prefer, green apple peel.

KEY INFORMATION

Common names: Garden sorrel, narrow-leaved dock, sorrel, spinach sorrel.

Botanical name: *Rumex acetosa*

Family: *Polygonaceae*

Parts used: Flowers, stems, leaves, and seeds.

DISTRIBUTION

Most of Europe and Asia. Introduced to North America.

HABITAT

Meadows, by streams and in open places in woodland. Often found as a weed of acid soils.

How to Identify Sorrel

Sorrel is a slender herbaceous perennial plant about 60 centimetres high, it has tasty, juicy stems and edible, arrow-shaped leaves. Sorrel can be difficult to find before it flowers as it grows a small basal rosette of green leaves and can easily be overlooked amongst the grass.

The basal leaves are arrow-shaped, and 7 to 10 cm long, with long petioles. Leaves on the flower stems are smaller and sessile, with their arrow "tails" wrapped around the stem. All the leaves taste sour, like green apple peel.

The flowers are whorled spikes of red flowers which bloom in early summer, become darker almost purple over time. The plant is dioecious, with male and female flowers on different plants. When still young, the flowers also taste sour.

The seeds are tiny, red winged seeds that are carried easily on the wind.

Sorrel seed head

Food

The leaves can be eaten raw or cooked. Please read the Known Hazards section before consuming raw sorrel in large quantities. The leaves make a thirst-quenching snack (the sour flavour encourages mouth watering). They can be added to salads, and used as a potherb or in soups. Depending on local conditions, the leaves can be available throughout the winter.

The flowers can also be eaten raw or cooked. The flowers can be cooked along with the leaves, or used as a garnish.

The seed can be used raw or cooked. The seeds can be ground into a flour and mixed with other wild flours, however, although the seeds are easy to harvest in large quantities, they are very small and fiddly to handle.

Medicine

The leaves can be used to make a cooling drink in the treatment of fevers. An infusion of the root is astringent, and diuretic. Grieve's "A Modern Herbal" (Note: written in 1931) claims that it has been used in the treatment of jaundice, gravel and kidney stones, but given the current advice against consuming it if you are prone to kidney stones, I would strongly advise against it! A homeopathic remedy is made from the plant used in the treatment of spasms and skin ailments.

Known hazards

Sorrel leaves can contain quite high levels of oxalic acid, which is what gives it the lovely green apple peel flavour, and it is perfectly alright to eat in small quantities; However, anyone with rheumatism, arthritis, gout, kidney stones, hyperacidity, cystitis or interstitial cystitis should avoid all but a taste of this plant as it could aggravate their conditions.

In large quantities, oxalic acid kind bind to other dietary nutrients, especially calcium, and make them unavailable for use by the body, potentially causing mineral deficiencies, so try not to gorge on big bowls full of the stuff!

HARVESTING

Leaves are best in spring and summer, but can still be available through autumn and winter too. They can be dried for later use, but lose some of their sourness.

POTENTIAL LOOKALIKES

The leaves are a similar shape to bindweed (*Convolvulus arvensis*), but this grows as a sprawling, long plant whereas sorrel grows as a rosette.

The biggest danger for anyone looking for sorrel, is that you get impatient and start trying leaves that look a bit like sorrel's description. Young Arum leaves can look quite similar if you've never seen sorrel before, but even the tiniest taste of Arum can cause great discomfort. Please do your research, and as always if you're not 100% sure, don't put it in your mouth!

Scarlet Elf Cups (*Sarcoscypha austriaca*)

When you see a scarlet elf cup, you'll know where the name comes from straight away. White on the outside and bright red in its inverted cup-like cap, it would make an ideal drink holder for an elf.

Key information

Common names: Moss cups, red cup, scarlet cup, scarlet elf cap.

Botanical name: *Sarcoscypha austriaca*

Family: *Sarcoscyphacea*

Parts used: Cap and stipe.

Distribution

Widely distributed in the Northern Hemisphere, has been found in Africa, Asia, Europe, North and South America, and Australia.

Habitat

Sarcoscypha austriaca grows on decaying woody material from various plants: the rose family, beech, hazel, willow, elm. The fruit bodies of *S. austriaca* are often found growing singly or clustered in groups on buried or partly buried sticks in deciduous forests.

I've mostly found them mainly growing on damp ground in Birch stands.

How to identify Scarlet elf cups

The cup-shaped fruit bodies are usually produced during the cooler months of winter and early spring. The brilliant red interior of the cups—from which both the common and scientific names are derived—contrasts with the lighter-coloured exterior.

The cap is initially spherical, later shallowly saucer- or cup-shaped with rolled-in rims, and measure 2–5 cm in diameter. The inner surface of the cup is deep red (fading to orange when dry) and smooth, while the outer surface is whitish and covered with a dense matted layer of tiny hairs (a tomentum).

The stipe, when present, is stout and up to 4 cm long (if deeply buried) by 0.3–0.7 cm thick, and whitish, with a tomentum.

Food

The species is said to be edible, inedible, or "not recommended", depending on the author. Although its insubstantial fruit body and low numbers do not make it particularly suitable for the table, one source claims "children in the Jura are said to eat it raw on bread and butter; and one French author suggests adding the cups, with a little Kirsch, to a fresh fruit salad." The fruit bodies have been noted to be a source of food for rodents in the winter, and slugs in the summer.

I've blended them with Judas' Ears, Black Oysters and Hairy bittercress, with a little stock to make a lovely soup; presented with a Scarlet elf cup floating on top. I also consider them to be one the few fungi in the UK which is edible raw, however, it's generally considered best to cook all wild mushrooms.

Medicine

Sarcoscypha austriaca was used as a medicinal fungus by the Oneida Indians, and possibly by other tribes of the Iroquois Six Nations. The fungus, after being dried and ground up into a powder, was applied as a styptic, particularly to the navels of newborn children that were not healing properly after the umbilical cord had been severed. Pulverized fruit bodies were also kept under bandages made of soft-tanned deerskin.

Known hazards

None known.

Harvesting

Late winter to early spring is the best time to find these.

Potential lookalikes

There is the very similar Ruby elf cup (*S. coccinea*) which is almost impossible to tell the difference with the naked eye, however it has the same edible properties and flavour.

Next Steps

So what happens now? You've read through the book, maybe you've got out and had a little practice identifying and tasting the plants and fungi, and you're wondering what the next steps for a budding forager are.

If you're looking for more seasonal plant profiles, you'll find more in the companion guides:

- Foraging for Wild Food in England – Summer edition, and
- Foraging for Wild Food in England – Autumn edition

If you're looking for inspiration for how to use your foraged bounty, we've created a companion cookbook:

- Foraging for Wild Food in England – Cookbook

And you can order them from here:
https://foundfood.com/shop/publications/

If you want to develop your knowledge even further, there is The Forager Helper, which is a web resource full of plant and fungi monographs, recipes, videos etc. which can be found at
www.foundfood.com/forager-helper

If you're starting to come across botanical terminology and you'd like some help with the scientific names, leaf and flowers structures, plant lifecycles, and other scientific words and concepts, the The Forager's Introduction to Botany is for you. You can find it here:
https://shop.foundfood.com/products/the-foragers-guide-to-botany

There's one experience which tops all of the products, and that's getting out there with a professional forager teacher. You can find my schedule here if you'd like some face-to-face learning:
https://foundfood.com/public-events/

About the Author

Gavin is passionate about understanding how plants and fungi live and work and how we can use them to our benefit without causing harm to the environment. Having had a very 'outdoors' childhood in the 1970s, Gavin spent ten years serving in the British Army where he learned about emergency food and first aid (including the beginnings of foraging and herbalism). After a second (third?) career in IT, Gavin reignited his passion for the natural world and started studying foraging in earnest. One thing led to another and before you know it he's studying herbalism and botany too, and running regular walks in and around London to introduce others to the fascinating world all around us.

Gavin formed FoundFood.com in 2012 as a personal database of his learnings, so he would always be able to look up where he had learned something from. In 2017 FoundFood.com became a blog to share some foraging related musings and experiences, them in 2023 Gavin started making his database of foraging information available to subscribers, and it has continued to grow ever since.

Now, in 2024, after many requests, Gavin has begun to release online courses and books available from www.foundfood.com